A Snail Mail Guide to Cursive Writing Practice

CHRISTINE RICHARDS

Snail Mail:
paper mail delivered by a postal system

Dedicated to my ever brilliant and supportive mother who sat me down, alongside my brothers and sisters, to write thank you notes to our equally brilliant and supportive grandparents.

I marveled then, as I do now, at how we can put words on paper, seal them in an envelope, and send them off.

Thank you.

Thank you to all the family, friends, and workshop participants who submitted handwriting samples. Though I couldn't include them all, each one is as unique as the person who wrote it.

©2020 / All rights reserved. No portion of this book may be used or reproduced in any manner without written permission except for brief quotations in articles or reviews.

Composition1206 LLC
PO Box 5290
Portland, ME 04101

ISBN 978-0-578-79509-6

A Snail Mail Guide to Cursive Writing Practice

CHRISTINE RICHARDS

What's Inside

1 ### Introduction • 1
It's a winning combination. Write letters to spend more time with the people you love and like best and improve your handwriting at the same time.

2 ### Snail Mail: Getting Started • 3
Say hello to friends and family—with a letter. Inside you'll find tips for who to write to and what to write about.

3 ### Elements of a Letter • 12
Not sure where to start? This diagram shows you how to set up your letter and address the envelope.

4 ### *I Write Letters to Say* • 15
The *I Write Letters to Say* section pulls sentences from real letters. Each page features a handwriting sample and space for you to practice your own handwriting.

5 ### Cursive Writing • 29
From A-Z these pages have step-by-step cursive writing instruction for each letter of the alphabet.

6 ### 10 Reasons to Write a Letter • 47
There are probably more than 10 reasons to write, here's a start.

Introduction

A winning combination

It's hard being apart from the people you love and like best. Texts, phone calls, and social media are great, but sometimes it's just not enough.

How can you bring them closer? Write a letter. An old-fashioned pen-on-paper letter—and mail it.

Write to someone you love, someone you like, someone who did something nice for you. Write about what's happening in the neighborhood, that project you finally finished, the rain pelting the window, your morning walk, the cookies you baked, or the book you're reading.

But wait. Are you embarrassed by your handwriting? Was your school one of the schools that cut cursive writing from the curriculum? Maybe it's been a while since you wrote—well, anything—and you're just a bit rusty.

That's how it is for a lot of us.

A Snail Mail Guide to Cursive Writing Practice will show you how to structure a letter, figure out who to write to (and what to write about), and help you improve your handwriting at the same time.

No, it won't replace a hug or a conversation across the kitchen table. But snail mail does give people something to hold onto.

Are you ready? Let's write.

— *Chrissy*

Snail Mail: Getting Started

Another way to say hello

You might wonder how to start a letter or what to write about. And you might think you need to be clever or write about some grand adventure.

The truth is, you don't need to be clever or adventurous. Unless, of course, you are. You just need to be you.

- Write about the things you see and the things you do.

- Write as if you're talking to the person you're writing to. What would you talk about?

- Sometimes, starting your letter on a piece of scratch paper can help. Say out loud what you might talk about and write it down. Or write a list of words and topics you could write about. Turn them into sentences. Cross out what you don't like, rearrange things, and copy what you've got onto a sheet of stationery or inside a blank card.

And relax. Letter writing is all about connecting with people. Your letters are not school papers, no one will be grading you, so try to have some fun with it.

When you're ready to send your letter, you may (like me), feel the butterflies in your stomach flutter a bit. That's OK. Sending a letter on its way takes courage. Just remember, people love getting mail—they really do.

36104	When I **MAIL** something,	08608
99801	I like to *imagine*,	87501
85001	a few days later,	12207
72201	that certain	27601
95814	**someone**	58501
80202	eyeing something	43215
06103	**curious**	73102
19901	in the mail bin,	97301
32301	picking it up and	17101
30303	holding it, ever so	02903
96813	briefly, just a bit	29217
83702	**closer.**	57501

When I **MAIL** something, I like to *imagine*, a few days later, that certain **someone** eyeing something **curious** in the mail bin, picking it up and holding it, ever so briefly, just a bit **closer.**

36104 99801 85001 72201 95814 80202 06103 19901 32301 30303 96813 83702 62701 46225 50309 66603 40601 70802 04101 21401 02101 48933 55102 39205 65101 59623 68502 89701 03301

08608 87501 12207 27601 58501 43215 73102 97301 17101 02903 29217 57501 37219 73701 84111 05602 23219 98507 25301 53701 82001 20001

Who to write to?
Start with family and friends

Oh, they'll be so happy to hear from you—really, they will.

It doesn't matter if they live in the same town, the next state over, on the other side of the country, or some faraway place. Write to them.

Is there someone you miss? Send them a note and tell them so.

Do you and a friend share a hobby? Write and tell them what you're working on and tell them how it's going. Ask a question about what they're doing.

Know someone serving in the military? Members in all branches of service look forward to getting mail. If you know someone serving in the Air Force, Army, Navy, Coast Guard, Marine Corps, or National Guard, get their address and tell them you're thinking of them and share a story.

Do you know someone who's sick or sad or lonely? Share a short story and tell them you've been thinking about them, too.

Letter writing is a way to spend more time with people you love and like best. They may not write back, but writing can make you feel closer. And who knows—someone may surprise you and write back.

A Collection *of* Stamps

place stamp here

Tools of the Trade
Gather your materials

You'll have a better experience writing letters if you start by gathering your materials before you sit down to write.

Here's what you'll need:

- **your favorite pen or marker**

    (pencil can be hard to read, so use a pen or marker, especially on the envelope)

- **stationery** (a greeting card or writing sheets along with an envelope)

- **stamps** (Forever® stamps for letters, postcard stamps for postcards)

- **the address of the person you're writing to**

- **scratch paper** (it's optional, but you can use scratch paper to practice writing what you want to say, and it can help you get started)

Stationery and Writing Papers

Buy some or make some

You've got lots of options when it comes to stationery and writing papers. There are expensive, lush papers available from high-end stationery stores and inexpensive papers and cards at discount stores.

And so many styles—silly cards with funny sayings, cards with flowers, photographs, and drawings. Choose what fits your budget—and your personality.

Or, make your own.

Another option is to use repurposed papers as stationery.

Here are some ideas:
- the backside of drawings and paintings you create
- paper wrappings from canned goods—like corn and beans and tomatoes
- decorative wrappers from fancy soaps
- paper from a deconstructed 5 lb. bag of flour or sugar (see page 48)
- cardboard from cereal boxes (great for postcards)
- coloring pages
- wrapping paper

Use what suits your budget and style.

Salutations & Closings
Saying hello and goodbye

The most common way to begin your letter is to start with "Dear," followed by the name of the person you're writing to. For example: Dear Susie, or Dear Grandpa.

There are others, of course, and the more familiar you are with the person you're writing to, the more casual you can be.

"Sincerely" is a common and polite way to close your letter. For those closest to you, "Love," may be appropriate—but certainly, not for all.

Here are some suggestions:

Salutations

Dear _____,
Hello _____,
Hi _____,
My love,
My dear _____,
Dearest _____,
Sweet _____,
Sweetheart,
Dear Friend,

Closings

Sincerely,
All the best,
Always,
With affection,
Respectfully,
Warm regards,
With gratitude,
Your friend,
Love,

Some salutations and closings may sound awkward if spoken, but when they are written, they can be quite touching.

Elements of a Letter

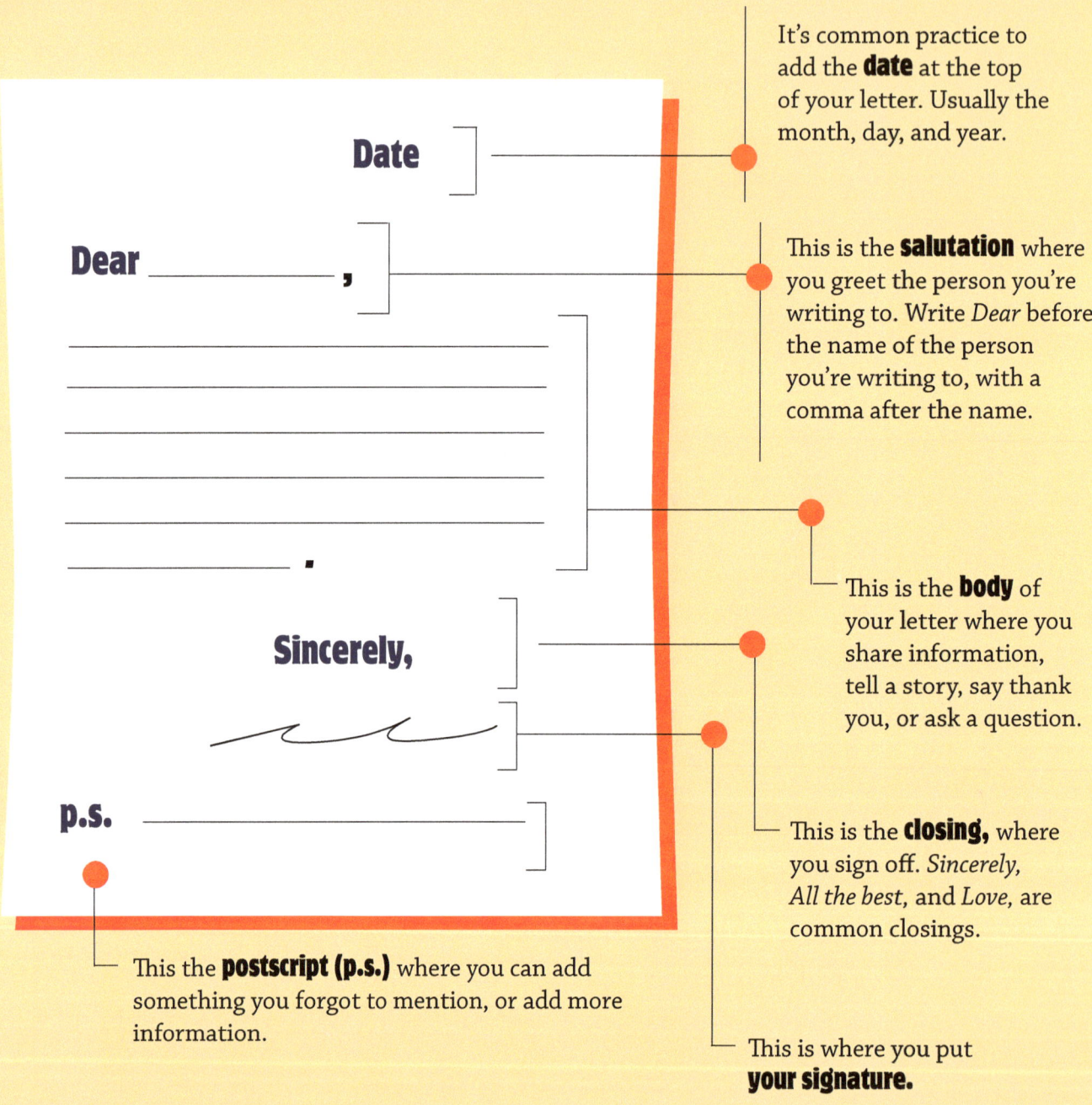

It's common practice to add the **date** at the top of your letter. Usually the month, day, and year.

This is the **salutation** where you greet the person you're writing to. Write *Dear* before the name of the person you're writing to, with a comma after the name.

This is the **body** of your letter where you share information, tell a story, say thank you, or ask a question.

This is the **closing,** where you sign off. *Sincerely, All the best,* and *Love,* are common closings.

This is where you put **your signature.**

This the **postscript (p.s.)** where you can add something you forgot to mention, or add more information.

• AL • AK • AR • AZ • CA • CO • CT • DC • DE • FL • GA • HI • IA •

• MS • MT • NC • ND • NE • NH • NJ • NM • NV • NY • OH • OK • OR •

The Envelope

This is the front of the envelope.

The side with the flap is the back of the envelope.

Your Name
Your Street Address
Your City, State, Zip Code

First and Last Name
Street Address
City, State, Zip Code

The stamp. The stamp is always placed in the upper right-hand corner of the envelope. It covers the fee for delivering first-class letters and cards weighing one ounce or less.

The return address. This is where you put your name and address.

This is the mailing address.
It sits in the center on the front of the envelope:
- **1st line:** The name of the person you're writing to.
- **2nd line:** Their full street name, avenue, or road, along with the building, apartment, suite, or floor number (this could take more than one line).
- **3rd line:** the city or town where the person lives, the state (using the two-letter state abbreviation), and the zip code.

ID • IL • IN • KS • KY • LA • MA • MD • ME • MI • MN • MO •

PA • RI • SC • SD • TN • TX • UT • VA • VT • WA • WI • WV • WY •

I Write Letters to Say
What to write about

Some of the best letters are the ones that start off with a statement. One line that captures your reader's attention.

On the following pages you'll find *I Write Letters to Say,* an illustrated series of sentences from real letters.

What is it about what you're writing that makes it most interesting? Use that as your first line.

When you compose your letters, use details.

Tell the person you're writing to about the super shiny eggplant you got at the farm stand. Don't just say dinner was delicious. Talk about how fluffy the mashed potatoes were. And if you write about the barking dog down the street, describe the dog. Call it a mutt if that's what it is. But if it's a prancing poodle, a graceful Great Dane, or baying basset, say so.

Without being sarcastic or insincere, have some fun with the words you choose.

Each *I Write Letters to Say* entry includes a short story with a handwriting sample. If you've never studied cursive writing, it can be difficult to read. These pages will help.

I write letters to say ...

At the corner of the block
near the stop sign

I saw a cat in the bushes

where the birds like to be.

I looked at the cat, the cat looked at me, and I'm pretty sure it gave me the stink eye.

I saw a cat in the bushes...

Your turn!

Copy the line in your own handwriting:

I write letters to say ...

It was chilly last night, and my feet were cold. So cold,

I wore socks to bed.

I wore socks to bed

Your turn!

Copy the line in your own handwriting:

A Snail Mail Guide to Cursive Writing Practice • 17

I write letters to say ...

The rain pelted the window

and like a lullaby, put me to sleep.

The rain pelted the window

Your turn!

Copy the line in your own handwriting:

I write letters to say ...

I stepped out of the neighborhood market and heard them. Two little girls riding their bicycles.

The girls were **giggling,** giggling, giggling, and pedaling, pedaling, **pedaling.**

The girls were giggling

Your turn!

Copy the line in your own handwriting:

I write letters to say ...

The man in front of me at the grocery store put a pumpkin on the counter.

He said he was going to make a pie.

He said he was going to make a pie.

Your turn!

Copy the line in your own handwriting:

I write letters to say ...

I see them every day, sometimes two or three times a day. They loop around the block no matter the weather. Today there was something different about them. It took me a minute to figure it out.

It was so cold even the dog wore a coat.

It was so cold even the dog wore a coat.

Your turn!

Copy the line in your own handwriting:

I write letters to say ...

The soup is on.

It's cold and damp today and I wanted something warm to eat, so I made soup.

The soup is on.

Your turn!

Copy the line in your own handwriting:

I write letters to say ...

This morning **I crossed paths** with the **scent** of a **lilac.**

I crossed paths with the scent of a lilac.

Your turn!

Copy the line in your own handwriting:

I write letters to say ...

Last night it was **breakfast for dinner.**

Last night it was breakfast for dinner.

Your turn!

Copy the line in your own handwriting:

I write letters to say ...

I go to the library to check out

of this world and into another.

I go to the library to Check out

Your turn!

Copy the line in your own handwriting:

I write letters to say ...

The acorns are falling and it's **an all-day buffet** for the **squirrels**.

an all-day buffet for the squirrels

Your turn!

Copy the line in your own handwriting:

I write letters to say ...

It's been overcast and gray. For days.
This morning the light shifted and sunlight
poured into the living room. I put my sneakers
on and took a walk. It was sunny,
then cloudy,
then sunny
again.

The **sun** was playing **peek-a-boo** with me.

The sun was playing peek-a-boo with me.

Your turn!

Copy the line in your own handwriting:

A Snail Mail Guide to Cursive Writing Practice

Cursive Writing

Five things to remember

Be it loopy and large, compact, or flourished, your handwriting is as personal and as unique as you are.

If you worry about your handwriting, or wonder if it's worth all the effort, here are five things to remember:

1) **Writing by hand can help you become a better thinker.** If something's got you stumped, worried, or perplexed, writing about it by hand can help you sort things out. If you're in school or taking a class, taking notes by hand can help you focus, learn, and remember more.

2) **Handwriting is a skill.** The more you practice the better it will get.

3) **Learning to write cursive will help you read cursive.** Because the thing is, if you haven't studied cursive writing it can be difficult to read.

4) **Your handwriting is like a special ring tone**—no one else's writing is quite like yours. It's the secret ingredient that makes your letters, cards, and notes so special.

5) **Don't fret if it's not perfect.** It's not suppose to be.

Warm-Up Exercises

It's important to relax when you write. Before you start practicing, scribble and doodle a bit to get your hand and fingers moving. Use the empty boxes to copy the doodles and create your own.

Grip, Posture, and Practice
Are you right-handed or left-handed?

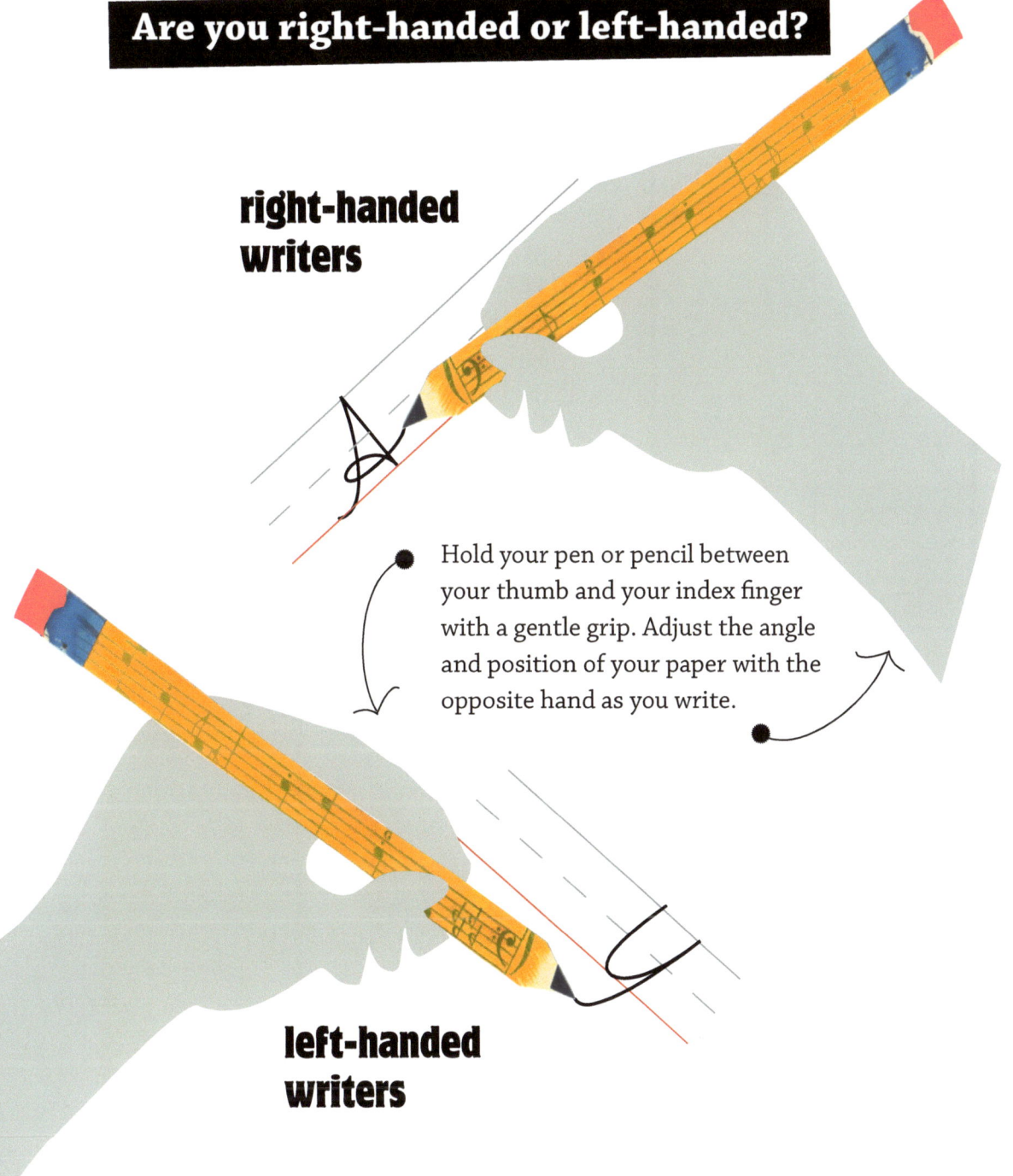

right-handed writers

Hold your pen or pencil between your thumb and your index finger with a gentle grip. Adjust the angle and position of your paper with the opposite hand as you write.

left-handed writers

Sit at a table or desk so that your wrist and arm rest comfortably on the surface, keep your back straight, and your feet flat on the floor.

Keep a loose grip. Use your opposite hand to adjust and keep your paper in place as you write.

The Alphabet

A a	*Aa*	N n	*Nn*
B b	*Bb*	O o	*Oo*
C c	*Cc*	P p	*Pp*
D d	*Dd*	Q q	*Qq*
E e	*Ee*	R r	*Rr*
F f	*Ff*	S s	*Ss*
G g	*Gg*	T t	*Tt*
H h	*Hh*	U u	*Uu*
I i	*Ii*	V v	*Vv*
J j	*Jj*	W w	*Ww*
K k	*Kk*	X x	*Xx*
L l	*Ll*	Y y	*Yy*
M m	*Mm*	Z z	*Zz*

Cursive writing is connected writing; one letter joining with the next. Though you may be familiar with the Palmer Method or some other cursive writing style, there is no one style that defines cursive writing. Some have more loops and curves than others.

The cursive alphabet in this book is a simplified style with fewer loops and strokes.

As your skill improves, you can modify the shape and style of your letters by adding loops and curves from the styles you prefer. Some variations for each letter of the alphabet are at the front and back of the book. As your cursive writing skills improve, experiment until you develop a style that suits you.

Each letter is written with one or more strokes. Start at the number one, red dot. Follow the red line in the direction of the arrows. Move to the number two and number three dots and do the same.

Trace over the gray letters and then write them on your own.

Aa Bb

Tip: The red line on the practice sheet is the **baseline.** Pay attention to how each letter sits on the baseline.

A Snail Mail Guide to Cursive Writing Practice • 33

Each letter is written with one or more strokes. Start at the number one, red dot. Follow the red line in the direction of the arrows. Move to the number two and number three dots and do the same.

Trace over the gray letters and then write them on your own.

Cc   Dd

Tip: Join letters by extending the exit stroke of one letter to begin the next without lifting your pen or pencil.

C c cab   D d dab

34 • A Snail Mail Guide to Cursive Writing Practice

Each letter is written with one or more strokes. Start at the number one, red dot. Follow the red line in the direction of the arrows. Move to the number two and number three dots and do the same.

Trace over the gray letters and then write them on your own.

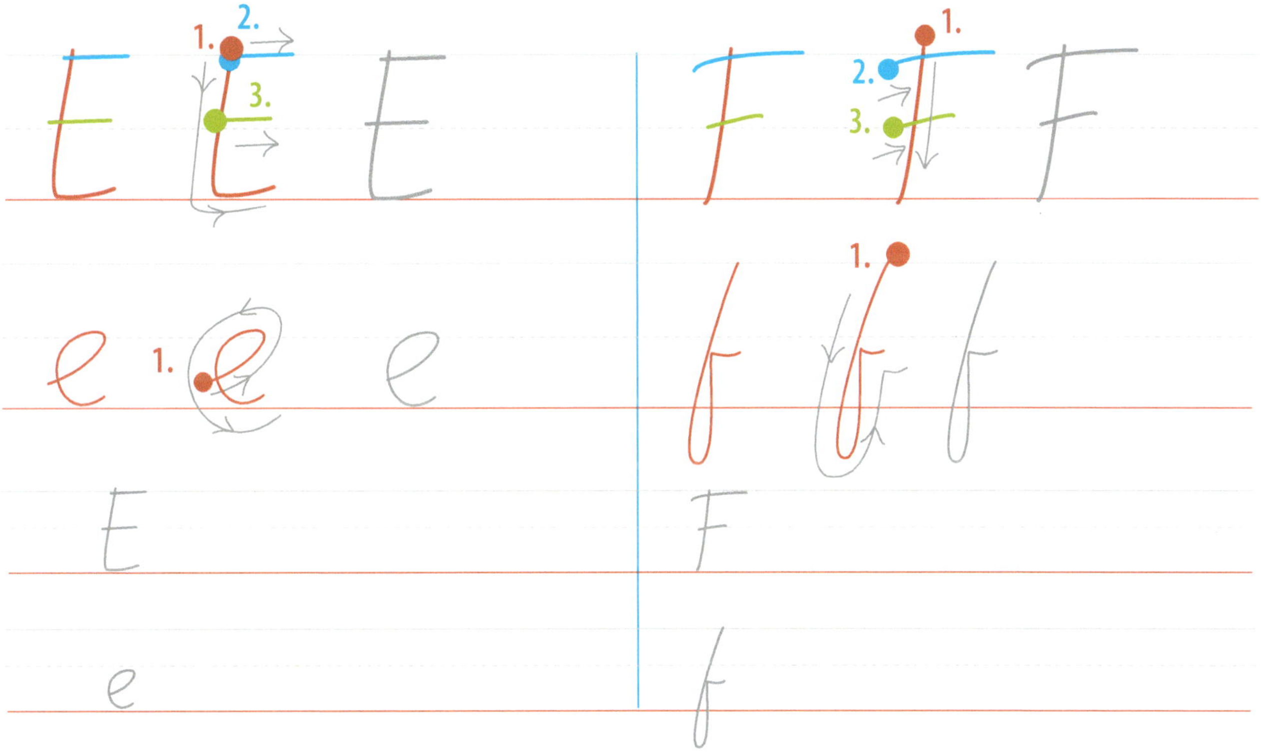

Tip: Experiment with the placement of your paper. Rotate it slightly to the left or right on the table top until you find a comfortable position.

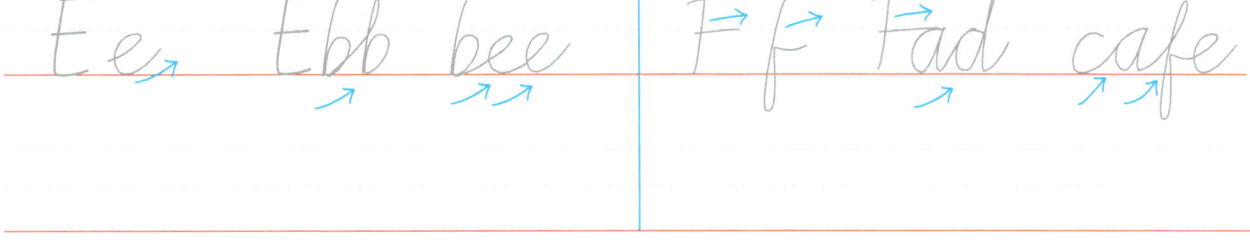

A Snail Mail Guide to Cursive Writing Practice • 35

Each letter is written with one or more strokes. Start at the number one, red dot. Follow the red line in the direction of the arrows. Move to the number two and number three dots and do the same.

Trace over the gray letters and then write them on your own.

Tip: If your hand hurts or you find you've got a tight grip on your pen or pencil, try holding it higher up, away from the point.

36 • A Snail Mail Guide to Cursive Writing Practice

Each letter is written with one or more strokes. Start at the number one, red dot. Follow the red line in the direction of the arrows. Move to the number two and number three dots and do the same.

Trace over the gray letters and then write them on your own.

Tip: As you write each word and move from one letter to another, ignore the dot over the i and the crossbar on the t and return to it once the entire word is written.

A Snail Mail Guide to Cursive Writing Practice • 37

Each letter is written with one or more strokes. Start at the number one, red dot. Follow the red line in the direction of the arrows. Move to the number two and number three dots and do the same.

Trace over the gray letters and then write them on your own.

Tip: Check the slant of your writing to be sure your letters are all leaning in the same direction.

38 • A Snail Mail Guide to Cursive Writing Practice

Each letter is written with one or more strokes. Start at the number one, red dot. Follow the red line in the direction of the arrows. Move to the number two and number three dots and do the same.

Trace over the gray letters and then write them on your own.

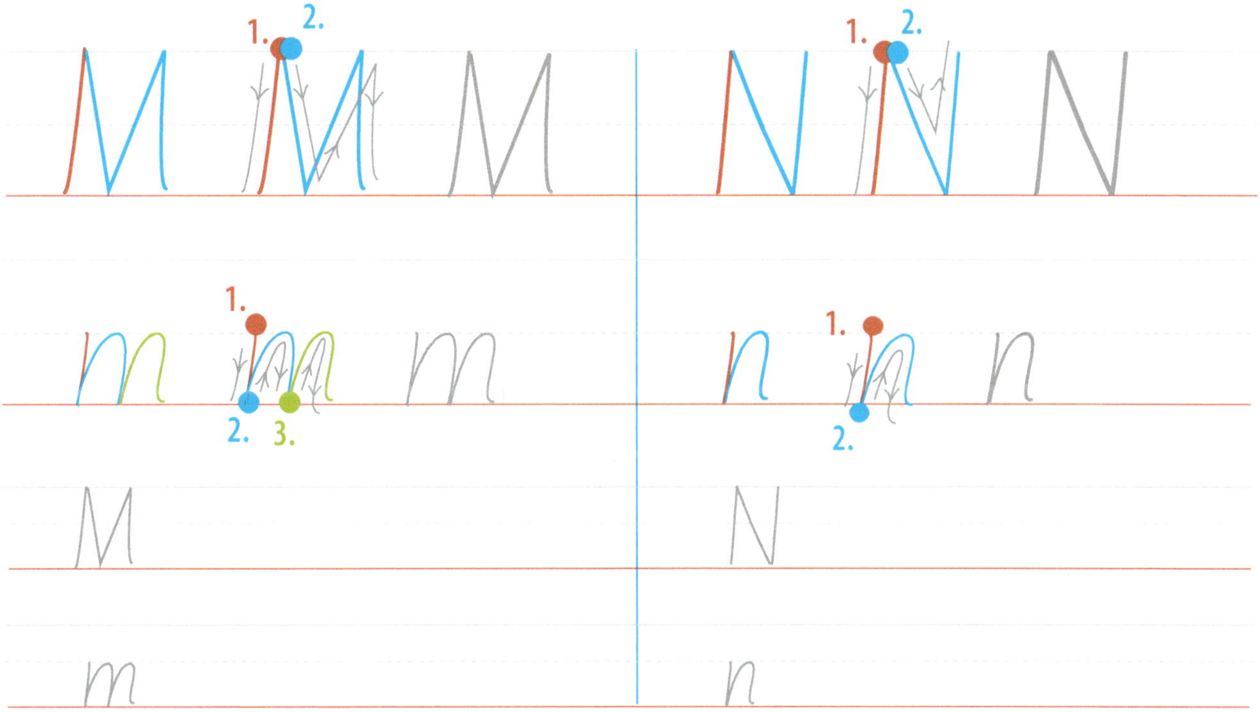

Tip: Not all letters need to be connected. If your hand gets tired, lift your pen or pencil and start the next letter without the connection.

A Snail Mail Guide to Cursive Writing Practice • 39

Each letter is written with one or more strokes. Start at the number one, red dot. Follow the red line in the direction of the arrows. Move to the number two and number three dots and do the same.

Trace over the gray letters and then write them on your own.

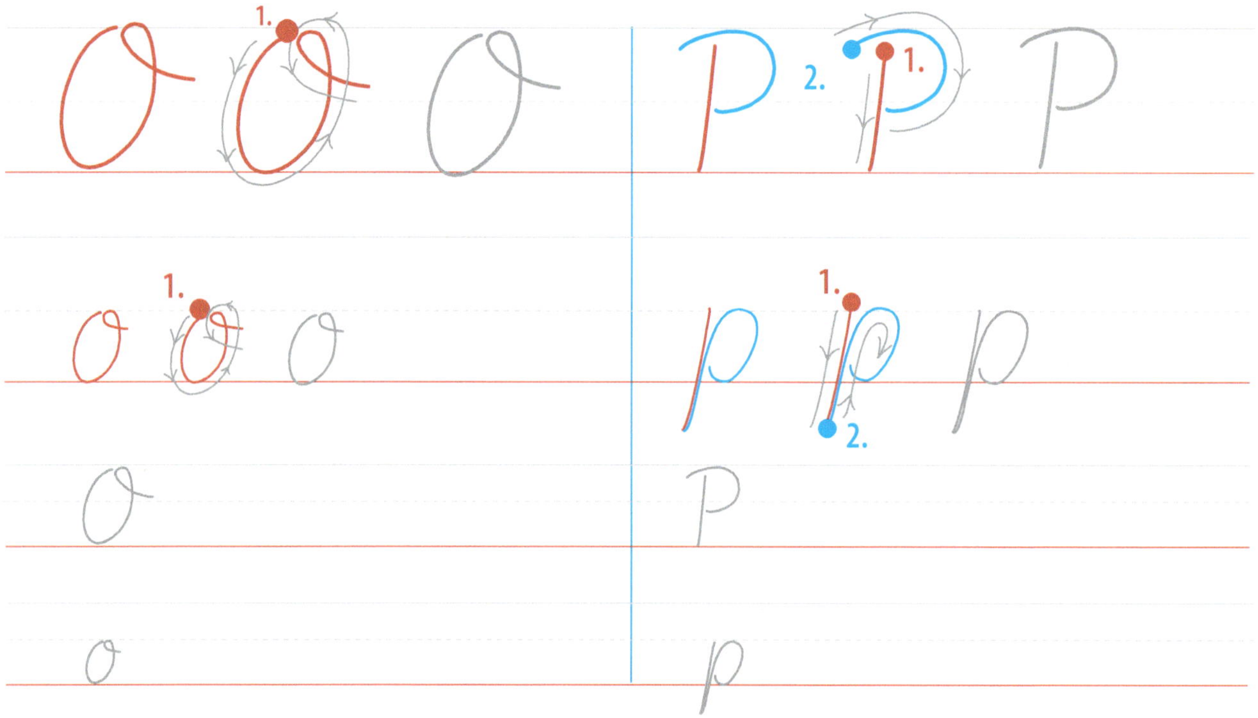

Tip: Adjust the position and angle of your paper as you write and move down the page.

40 • A Snail Mail Guide to Cursive Writing Practice

Each letter is written with one or more strokes. Start at the number one, red dot. Follow the red line in the direction of the arrows. Move to the number two and number three dots and do the same.

Trace over the gray letters and then write them on your own.

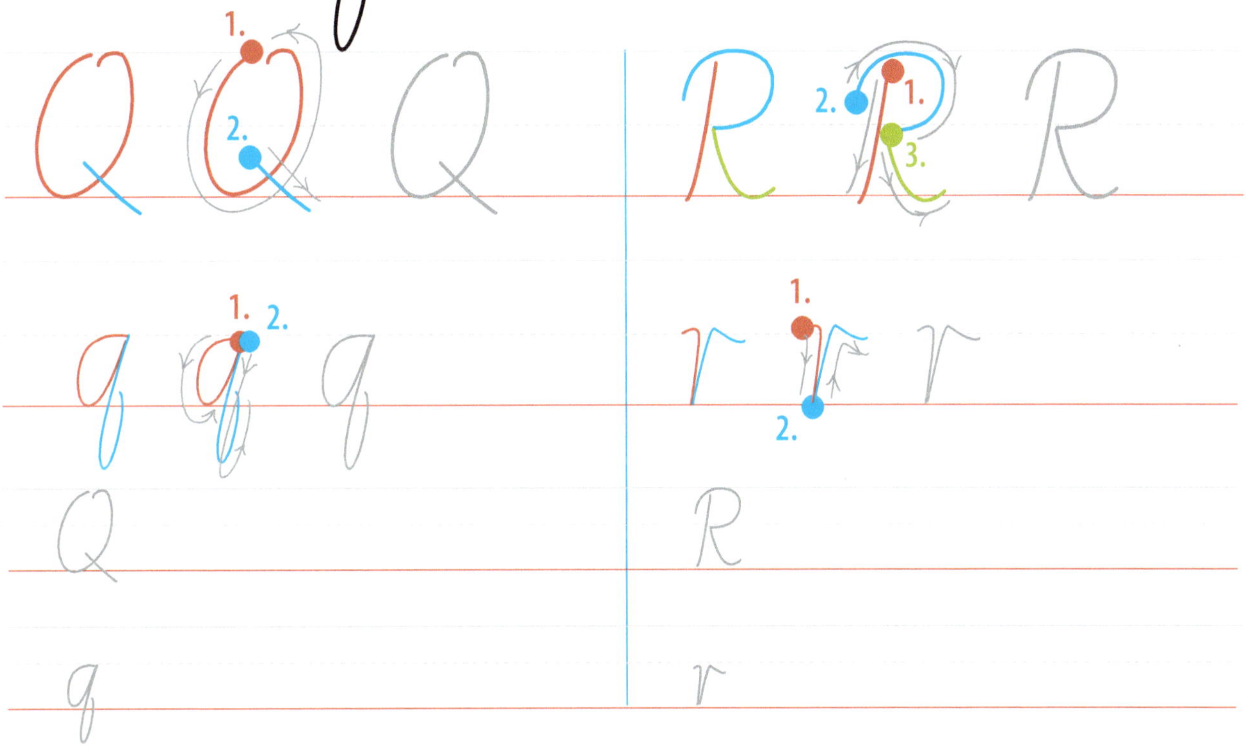

Tip: Check your posture as you write. Are you slumped over the table? Be sure to sit up straight and release any tension in your hand, neck, and back.

A Snail Mail Guide to Cursive Writing Practice • 41

Each letter is written with one or more strokes. Start at the number one, red dot. Follow the red line in the direction of the arrows. Move to the number two and number three dots and do the same.

Trace over the gray letters and then write them on your own.

Tip: Test different pens. You may find you have a preference for a gel pen, a ballpoint, or a felt-tip marker.

Each letter is written with one or more strokes. Start at the number one, red dot. Follow the red line in the direction of the arrows. Move to the number two and number three dots and do the same.

Trace over the gray letters and then write them on your own.

Tip: Don't worry if your handwriting isn't perfect. It's not suppose to be.

A Snail Mail Guide to Cursive Writing Practice • 43

Each letter is written with one or more strokes. Start at the number one, red dot. Follow the red line in the direction of the arrows. Move to the number two and number three dots and do the same.

Ww

Trace over the gray letters and then write them on your own.

Xx

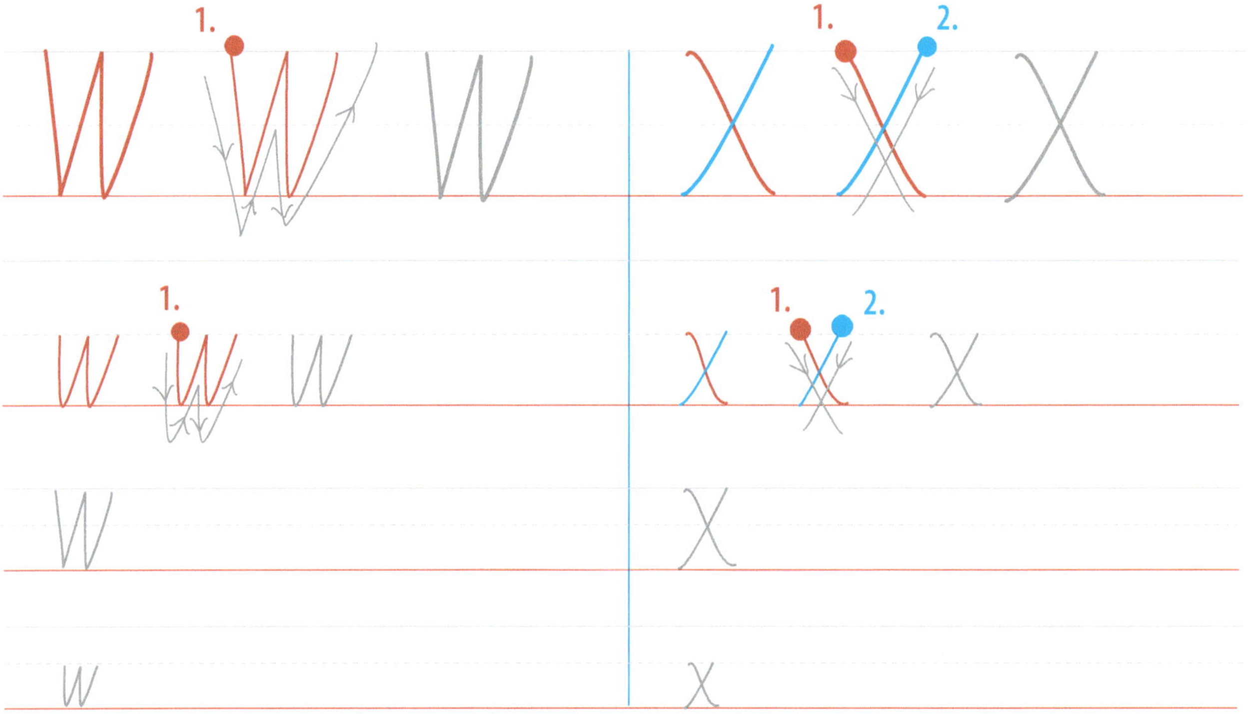

Tip: Experiment with different papers. Some papers have smooth surfaces that allow your pen to glide. Others have a rougher surface that can cause your pen to drag.

Ww We wrap Xx axe fox

Each letter is written with one or more strokes. Start at the number one, red dot. Follow the red line in the direction of the arrows. Move to the number two and number three dots and do the same.

Trace over the gray letters and then write them on your own.

Tip: Write and send letters, cards, and notes for practice. Remember, it's another way to say hello and spend more time with the people you like.

A Snail Mail Guide to Cursive Writing Practice

10 Reasons to Write a Letter

1. **Start a conversation.**
   Sometimes we don't have enough time with the people we love and like best. Writing allows us to spend more time together.

2. **Visit without traveling.**
   Being separated from friends and family can be tough. Social media is convenient, but there's something different about a letter—it gives people something to hold onto.

3. **Get to know one another.**
   Writing can help you get to know someone—you share your stories and they'll share theirs.

4. **Writing will give you a sense of accomplishment.**
   It can be scary to reach out and put your words on paper. The more you do it, though, the easier it gets. And with every letter you send, your courage grows.

5. **It can help you say things that matter.**
   What makes the people you care about so special? Are they funny? Do they sing to you, walk the dog, do the dishes, support and cheer you on? Write and tell them so.

6. **Express your creativity.**
   Aside from how you address the envelope, there are no rules. You can share stories, send poetry, decorate your stationery and envelopes with artwork, and experiment with your handwriting.

7. **The more you send the more you get.**
   Not always, but once in a while, if you write to someone, they'll write back.

8. **Mail makes people happy.**
   Getting mail is proof that someone's been thinking about you. And that? Well, that feels good.

9. **Your composition skills will improve.**
   With each letter you write, you'll get better at organizing your thoughts, choosing the right words, and putting sentences together.

10. **Your handwriting will improve.**
    Yes, it will—but you already knew that.

I once wrote a letter to my friend who is a baker. The note was on paper from a deconstructed 5 lb. bag of flour. **She had the perfect comeback:** a letter on paper from a 50 lb. bag of sugar—*sweet!*

N n O o P p Q q
N R r R T t
U u S s W
V v Y W w
X x Y y Z

www.ingramcontent.com/pod-product-compliance
Lightning Source LLC
Chambersburg PA
CBHW041202290426
44109CB00003B/108